The
Qur'ân
& Modern
Science

Compatible or Incompatible?

By Dr. Zakir Naik

Designed by: Abdul Hameed

DARUSSALAM

© **Maktaba Dar-us-Salam, 2007**

King Fahd National Library Catalog-in-Publication Data

Dr. Zakir Naik

The Quran and Modern Science. Zakir Naik - Riyadh. 2007

80 p, 14x21 cm   **ISBN: 9960-9849-3-1**

1-Quran and science   2- Quran - Miracle   I-Title

229.45 dc   1428/176

Legal Deposit no.1428/176

ISBN: 9960-9849-3-1

Supervised by: **Abdul Malik Mujahid**

HEAD OFFICE

P.O. Box: 22743, Riyadh 11416 K.S.A.Tel: 00966-1-4033962/4043432 Fax: 4021659
E-mail: darussalam@awalnet.net.sa, riyadh@dar-us-salam.com Website: www.dar-us-salam.com

K.S.A. Darussalam Showrooms:
Riyadh
Olaya branch: Tel 00966-1-4614483 Fax: 4644945
Malaz branch: Tel 00966-1-4735220 Fax: 4735221
Suwaydi: Tel: 00966 1 4286641
Suwailam branch: Tel & Fax-1-2860422
• Jeddah
  Tel: 00966-2-6879254 Fax: 6336270
• Madinah
  Tel: 00966-04-8234446, 8230038
  Fax: 04-8151121
• Al-Khobar
  Tel: 00966-3-8692900 Fax: 8691551
• Khamis Mushayt
  Tel & Fax: 00966-072207055
* Yanbu Al-Bahr Tel: 0500887341 Fax: 04-3908027
• Al-Buraida Tel: 0503417156 Fax: 06-3696124
U.A.E
• Darussalam, Sharjah U.A.E
  Tel: 00971-6-5632623 Fax: 5632624
  Sharjah@dar-us-salam.com.
PAKISTAN
• Darussalam, 36 B Lower Mall, Lahore
  Tel: 0092-42-724 0024 Fax: 7354072
• Rahman Market, Ghazni Street,Urdu Bazar Lahore
  Tel: 0092-42-7120054 Fax: 7320703
• Karachi, Tel: 0092-21-4393936 Fax: 4393937
• Islamabad, Tel: 0092-51-2500237 Fax: 512281513
U.S.A
• Darussalam, Houston
  P.O Box: 79194 Tx 77279
  Tel: 001-713-722 0419 Fax: 001-713-722 0431
  E-mail: houston@dar-us-salam.com
• Darussalam, New York 486 Atlantic Ave, Brooklyn
  New York-11217, Tel: 001-718-625 5925
  Fax: 718-625 1511
  E-mail: darussalamny@hotmail.com
U.K
• Darussalam International Publications Ltd.
  Leyton Business Centre
  Unit-17, Etloe Road, Leyton, London, E10 7BT
  Tel: 0044 20 8539 4885 Fax:0044 20 8539 4889
  Website: www.darussalam.com
  Email: info@darussalam.com
• Darussalam International Publications Limited
  Regents Park Mosque, 146 Park Road
  London NW8 7RG Tel: 0044- 207 725 2246
  Fax: 0044 20 8539 4889

AUSTRALIA
• Darussalam: 153, Haldon St, Lakemba (Sydney)
  NSW 2195, Australia
  Tel: 0061-2-97407188 Fax: 0061-2-97407199
  Mobile: 0061-414580813 Res: 0061-2-97580190
  Email: abumuaaz@hotamail.com
• The Islamic Bookstore
  Ground Floor-165 Haldon Street
  Lakemba, NSW 2195, Australia
  Tel: 0061-2-97584040 Fax: 0061-2-97584030
  Email: info@islamicbookstore.com.au
  Web Site: www.islamicbookstore.com.au
CANADA
• Nasiruddin Al-Khattab
  2-3415 Dixie Rd, Unit # 505
  Mississauga
  Ontario L4Y 4J6, Canada
  Tel: 001-416-418 6619
• Islamic Book Service
  2200 South Sheridan way Mississauga, On
  L5J 2M4
  Tel:001-905-403-8406 Ext. 218 Fax: 905-8409
FRANCE
• Editions & Librairie Essalam
  135, Bd de Ménilmontant- 75011 Paris
  Tél: 0033-01- 43 38 19 56/ 44 83
  Fax: 0033-01-43 57 44 31
  E-mail: essalam@essalam com·
MALAYSIA
• Darussalam
  Int'l Publishing & Distribution SDN BHD
  D-2-12, Setiawangsa 11, Taman Setiawangsa
  54200 Kuala Lumpur
  Tel: 03-42528200 Fax: 03-42529200
  Email: darussalam@streamyx.com
  Website: www.darussalam.com.my
SRI LANKA
• Darul Kitab 6, Nimal Road, Colombo-4
  Tel: 0094 115 358712 Fax: 115-358713
INDIA
• Islamic Books International
  54, Tandel Street (North)
  Dongri, Mumbai 4000   09, INDIA
  Tel: 0091-22-2373 4180
  E-mail: ibi@irf.net
SOUTH AFRICA
• Islamic Da'wah Movement (IDM)
  48009 Qualbert 4078 Durban,South Africa
  Tel: 0027-31-304-6883 Fax: 0027-31-305-1292
  E-mail: idm@ion.co.za

Contents

In the Name of Allâh, the Most Gracious, the Most Merciful

Introduction

Ever since the dawn of human life on this planet, Man has always sought to understand Nature, his own place in the scheme of Creation and the purpose of Life itself. In this quest for Truth, spanning many centuries and diverse civilizations, organized religion has shaped human life and determined to a large extent, the course of history. While some religions have been based on books, claimed by their adherents to be divinely inspired, others have relied solely on human experience.

Al-Qur'ân, the main source of the Islamic faith, is a book believed by Muslims, to be of completely Divine origin. Muslims also believe that it contains Divine guidance for all humankind. Since the message of the Qur'ân is believed to be for all times, it should be relevant to every age. Does the Qur'ân pass this test? In this booklet, I intend to give an objective analysis of the Muslim belief regarding the Divine origin of the Qur'ân, in the light of established scientific discoveries.

There was a time, in the history of world civilization, when 'miracles', or what was perceived to be a miracle, took precedence over human reason and logic. But how do we define the term 'miracle'? A miracle is anything that takes place out of the normal course of life and for which humankind has no explanation. However, we must be careful before we accept something as a miracle. An article in *'The Times of India',* Mumbai, in 1993 reported that 'a saint' by the name 'Baba Pilot' claimed to have stayed continuously submerged under water in a tank for three consecutive days and nights.

However, when reporters wanted to examine the base of the tank of water where he claimed to have performed this 'miraculous' feat, he refused to let them do so. He argued by asking as to how one could examine the womb of a mother that gives birth to a child. The 'Baba' was hiding something. It was a gimmick simply to gain publicity. Surely, no modern man with even the slightest inkling towards rational thinking would accept such a 'miracle'. If such false miracles are the tests of divinity, then we would have to accept Mr. P.C. Sorcar, the world famous magician known for his ingenious magical tricks and illusions, as the best god-man.

A book, claiming Divine origin, is in effect, claiming to be a miracle. Such a claim should be easily verifiable in any age, according to the standards of that age. Muslims believe, that the Qur'ân is the last and final revelation of God, the miracle of miracles revealed as a mercy to humankind. Let us therefore investigate the veracity of this belief.

1. I would like to thank Brother Musaddique Thange for his editorial assistance. May Allâh (﷾) reward him for his efforts. (*Âmin*)

The Qur'ân

The Challenge of the Qur'ân

Literature and poetry have been instruments of human expression and creativity, in all cultures. The world also witnessed an age when literature and poetry occupied pride of position, similar to that now enjoyed by science and technology.

Muslims as well as non-Muslims agree that the Qur'ân is Arabic literature par excellence – that it is the best Arabic literature on the face of the earth. The Qur'ân challenges mankind in the following Verses:

وَإِن كُنتُمْ فِي رَيْبٍ مِّمَّا نَزَّلْنَا عَلَىٰ عَبْدِنَا فَأْتُوا۟ بِسُورَةٍ مِّن مِّثْلِهِۦ وَٱدْعُوا۟ شُهَدَآءَكُم مِّن دُونِ ٱللَّهِ إِن كُنتُمْ صَـٰدِقِينَ ۝ فَإِن لَّمْ تَفْعَلُوا۟ وَلَن تَفْعَلُوا۟ فَٱتَّقُوا۟ ٱلنَّارَ ٱلَّتِى وَقُودُهَا ٱلنَّاسُ وَٱلْحِجَارَةُ ۖ أُعِدَّتْ لِلْكَـٰفِرِينَ ۝

And if ye are in doubt as to what We have revealed from time to time to our servant then produce a surah like thereunto; and call your witnesses or helpers (If there are any) besides Allah, if ye are truthful. But if ye cannot and of a surety ye cannot then fear the Fire whose fuel is Men and Stones, which is prepared for those who reject Faith. (Al-Qur'ân 2:23-24) [1]

The challenge of the Qur'ân, is to produce a single *Sûrah* (chapter) like the *Sûrahs* it contains. The same challenge is repeated in the Qur'ân several times. The challenge to produce a *Sûrah,* which, in beauty, eloquence, depth and

---

1. Al-Qur'ân 2:23-24 indicates *Surah* or Chapter No. 2 and *Âyât* or Verses 23 and 24. The same notation is followed throughout the book. References and translation of the Qur'ân are from the translation of the Holy Qur'ân by Abdullah Yusuf Ali, published by King Fahd Holy Qur'ân Printing Complex, Al-Madinah, Saudi Arabia.

meaning is at least somewhat similar to a Qur'ânic *Sûrah* remains unmet to this day.

A modern rational man, however, would never accept a religious scripture which says, in the best posssible poetic language, that the world is flat. This is because we live in an age, where human reason, logic and science are given primacy. Not many would accept the Qur'an's extraordinarily beautiful language, as proof of its Divine origin. Any scripture claiming to be a divine revelation must also be acceptable on the strength of its own reason and logic.

According to the famous physicist and Nobel Prize winner, Albert Einstein, "Science without religion is lame. Religion without science is blind." Let us therefore study the Qur'ân, and analyze whether the Qur'ân and Modern Science are compatible or incompatible?

The Qur'ân is not a book of science but a book of 'signs', i.e. *Âyâts*. There are more than six thousand 'signs' in the Qur'ân of which more than a thousand deal with science.

We all know that many a times science takes a 'U-turn'. In this book I have considered only established scientific facts and not mere hypotheses and theories that are based on assumptions and are not backed by proof.

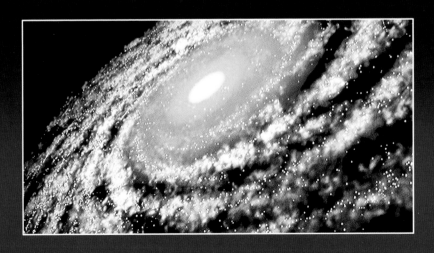

Creation of the Universe

The 'Big Bang'

The creation of the universe is explained by astrophysicists in a widely accepted phenomenon, popularly known as the 'Big Bang'. It is supported by observational and experimental data gathered by astronomers and astrophysicists for decades. According to the 'Big Bang', the whole universe was initially one big mass (Primary Nebula). Then there was a 'Big Bang' (Secondary Separation) which resulted in the formation of galaxies. These then divided to form stars, planets, the sun, the moon, etc. The origin of the universe was unique and the probability of its occurring by 'chance' is zero.

The Qur'ân contains the following verse, regarding the origin of the universe:

أَوَلَمۡ يَرَ ٱلَّذِينَ كَفَرُوٓاْ أَنَّ ٱلسَّمَٰوَٰتِ وَٱلۡأَرۡضَ كَانَتَا رَتۡقٗا فَفَتَقۡنَٰهُمَاۖ

Do not the Unbelievers see that the heavens and the earth were joined together (as one unit of Creation), before We clove them asunder? (Al-Qur'ân 21:30)

The striking congruence between the Qur'ânic verse and the 'Big Bang' is inescapable! How could a book, which first appeared in the deserts of Arabia 1400 years ago, contain this profound scientific truth?

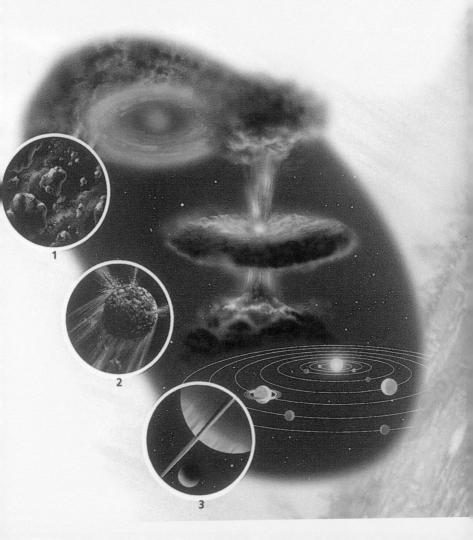

There was an Initial Gaseous Mass before the Creation of Galaxies

Scientists say that before the galaxies in the universe were formed, celestial matter was initially in the form of gaseous matter. In short, huge gaseous matter or clouds were present before the formation of the galaxies. To describe initial celestial matter, the word 'smoke' is more appropriate than gas. The following Qur'ânic verse refers to this state of the universe by the word *Dukhân* which means smoke.

ثُمَّ ٱسْتَوَىٰٓ إِلَى ٱلسَّمَآءِ وَهِيَ دُخَانٌ فَقَالَ لَهَا وَلِلْأَرْضِ ٱئْتِيَا طَوْعًا أَوْ كَرْهًا قَالَتَآ أَتَيْنَا طَآئِعِينَ ۝

Then He turned to the sky, and it had been (as) smoke: He said to it and to the earth: "Come ye together, willingly or unwillingly." They said: "We do come (together), in willing obedience." (Al-Qur'ân 41:11)

Again, this fact is a corollary to the 'Big Bang' and was not known to the Arabs during the time of Prophet Muhammad (ﷺ). What then, could have been the source of this knowledge?

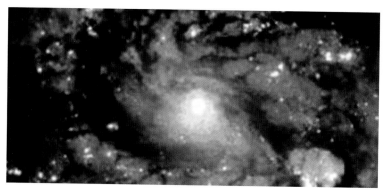

The Spherical Shape of the Earth

In early times, people believed that the earth is flat. For centuries, men were afraid to venture out too far, lest they should fall off the edge. Sir Francis Drake was the first person who proved that the earth is spherical when he sailed around it in 1577.

Consider the following Qur'ânic verse regarding the alternation of day and night:

أَلَمْ تَرَ أَنَّ ٱللَّهَ يُولِجُ ٱلَّيْلَ فِى ٱلنَّهَارِ وَيُولِجُ ٱلنَّهَارَ فِى ٱلَّيْلِ

Seest thou not that Allah merges Night into Day and He merges Day into Night.. (Al-Qur'ân 31:29)

Merging here means that the night slowly and gradually changes to day and vice versa. This phenomenon can only take place if the earth is spherical. If the earth was flat, there would have been a sudden change from night to day and from day to night.

The following verse also alludes to the spherical shape of the earth:

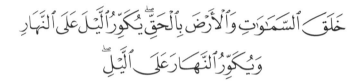

He created the heavens and the earth in true (proportions): He makes the Night overlap the Day, and the Day overlap the Night.. (Al-Qur'ân 39:5)

The Arabic word used here is *Kawwara* meaning 'to overlap' or 'to coil' – the way a turban is wound around the head. The overlapping or coiling of the day and night can take place if the earth is spherical.

The earth is not exactly round like a ball, but geo-spherical, i.e., it is flattened at the poles. The following verse contains a description of the earth's shape:

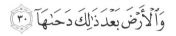

And the earth, moreover, hath He extended (to a wide expanse). (Al-Qur'ân 79:30)

The Arabic word for egg here is *Dahaha*[1] which means an ostrich-egg. The shape of an ostrich-egg resembles the geo-spherical shape of the earth.

Thus the Qur'ân correctly describes the shape of the earth, though the prevalent notion when the Qur'ân was revealed was that the earth is flat.

The Light of the Moon is Reflected Light

It was believed by earlier civilizations that the moon emanates its own light. Science now tells us that the light of the moon is reflected light. However this fact was mentioned in the Qur'ân 1,400 years ago in the following verse:

تَبَارَكَ ٱلَّذِى جَعَلَ فِى ٱلسَّمَآءِ بُرُوجًا وَجَعَلَ فِيهَا سِرَٰجًا وَقَمَرًا مُّنِيرًا ﴿٦١﴾

---

1. The Arabic word *Dahaha* has been translated by A. Yusuf Ali as 'vast expanse', which is also correct. The word *Dahaha* also means an ostrich-egg.

Blessed is He Who made constellations in the skies, and placed therein a lamp and a moon giving light. (Al-Qur'ân 25:61)

The Arabic word for the sun in the Qur'ân, is *Shams*. It is referred to as *Sirâj* which means a 'torch' or as *Wahhâj* which means 'a blazing lamp' or as *Diya* which means 'shining glory'. All three descriptions are appropriate to the sun, since it generates intense heat and light by its internal combustion. The Arabic word for the moon is *Qamar* and it is described in the Qur'ân as *Muneer* which is a body that gives *Noor*, i.e., light. Again, the Qur'ânic description matches perfectly with the true nature of the moon which does not give off light itself and is an inert body that reflects the light of the sun. Not once in the Qur'ân, is the moon mentioned as *Sirâj, Wahhâj* or *Diya* or the sun *as Noor* or *Muneer*. This implies that the Qur'ân recognizes the difference between the nature of sunlight and moonlight.

Consider the following verses related to the nature of light from the sun and the moon:

أَلَمْ تَرَوْاْ كَيْفَ خَلَقَ ٱللَّهُ سَبْعَ سَمَٰوَٰتٍ طِبَاقًا ۝ وَجَعَلَ ٱلْقَمَرَ فِيهِنَّ نُورًا وَجَعَلَ ٱلشَّمْسَ سِرَاجًا ۝

" 'See ye not how Allah has created the seven heavens one above another. And made the moon a light in their midst, and made the sun as a (glorious) lamp? (Al-Qur'ân 71:15-16)

The Sun rotates

For a long time European philosophers and scientists believed that the earth stood still in the center of the universe and every other body including the sun moved around it. In the West, this geocentric concept of the universe was prevalent right from the time of Ptolemy in the second century BC. In 1512, Nicholas Copernicus put forward his Heliocentric Theory of Planetary Motion, which asserted that the sun is motionless at the centre of the solar system with the planets revolving around it.

In 1609, the German scientist Johannes Kepler published the *'Astronomia Nova'*. In this he concluded that not only do the planets move in elliptical orbits around the sun, they also rotate upon their axes at irregular speeds. With this knowledge it became possible for European scientists to explain correctly many of the mechanisms of the solar system including the sequence of night and day.

After these discoveries, it was thought that the sun was stationary and did not rotate about its axis like the earth. I remember having studied this fallacy from geography books during my school days.

Consider the following Qur'ânic Verse:

> It is He Who created the night and the day, and the sun and the moon: All (the celestial bodies) swim along, each in its rounded course.   (Al-Qur'ân 21:33)

The Arabic word used in the above Verse is *Yasbahûn*. The word *Yasbahûn* is derived from the word *Sabaha*. It carries with it the idea of motion that comes from any moving body. If you use the word for a man on the ground, it would not mean that he is rolling but would mean he is walking or running. If you use the word for a man in water it would not mean that he is floating but would mean that he is swimming.

Similarly, if you use the word *Yasbah* for a celestial body such as the sun it would not mean that it is only flying through space but would mean that it is also rotating as it goes through space. Most of the school textbooks have incorporated the fact that the sun rotates about its axis. The rotation of the sun about its own axis can be proved with the help of an equipment that projects the image of the sun on the table top so that one can examine the image of the sun without being blinded. It is noticed that the sun has spots which complete a circular motion once every 25 days, i.e., the sun takes approximately 25 days to rotate around its axis.

In fact, the sun travels through space at roughly 150 miles per second, and takes about 200 million years to complete one revolution around the center of our Milky Way Galaxy.

لَا ٱلشَّمْسُ يَنۢبَغِى لَهَآ أَن تُدْرِكَ ٱلْقَمَرَ وَلَا ٱلَّيْلُ سَابِقُ ٱلنَّهَارِ ۚ وَكُلٌّ فِى فَلَكٍ يَسْبَحُونَ ﴿٤٠﴾

It is not permitted to the sun to catch up the moon, nor can the night outstrip the day: Each (just) swims along in (its own) orbit (According to Law). (Al-Qur'ân 36:40)

This verse mentions an essential fact discovered by modern astronomy, i.e., the existence of the individual orbits of the sun and the moon, and their journey through space with their own motion.

The 'fixed place' towards which the sun travels, carrying with it the solar system, has been located exactly by modern astronomy. It has been given a name, the Solar Apex. The solar system is indeed moving in space towards a point situated in the constellation of Hercules (alpha Lyrae) whose exact location is firmly established.

The moon rotates around its axis in the same duration that it takes to revolve around the earth. It takes approximately 29½ days to complete one rotation.

One cannot help but be amazed at the scientific accuracy of the Qur'ânic verses. Should we not ponder over the question: "What was the source of knowledge contained in the Qur'ân?"

The Sun will Extinguish after a Certain Period

The light of the sun is due to a chemical process on its surface that has been taking place continuously for the past five billion years. It will come to an end at some point of time in the future when the sun will be totally extinguished leading to extinction of all life on earth. Regarding the impermanence of the sun's existence the Qur'ân says:

And the sun runs unto a resting place, for him: that is the decree of (Him), the Exalted in Might, the All-Knowing[1]. (Al-Qur'ân 36:38)

The Arabic word used here is *Mustaqarr,* which means a place or time that is determined. Thus the Qur'ân says that the sun runs towards a determined place, and will do so only up to a pre-determined period of time- meaning that it will end or extinguish.

---

1. A similar message is conveyed in the Qur'ân in 13:2, 35:13, 39:5 and 31:29.

The Presence of Interstellar Matter

Space outside organized astronomical systems was earlier assumed to be a vacuum. Astrophysicists later discovered the presence of bridges of matter in this interstellar space. These bridges of matter are called plasma, and consist of completely ionized gas containing equal number of free electrons and positive ions. Plasma is sometimes called the fourth state of matter (besides the three known states, viz., solid, liquid and gas). The Qur'ân mentions the presence of this interstellar material in the following verse:

ٱلَّذِى خَلَقَ ٱلسَّمَٰوَٰتِ وَٱلْأَرْضَ وَمَا بَيْنَهُمَا

He Who created the heavens and the earth and all that is between. (Al-Qur'ân 25:59)

It would be ridiculous, for anybody to even suggest that the presence of interstellar galactic material was known 1400 years ago.

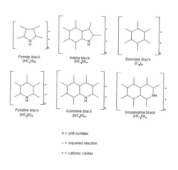

The Expanding Universe

In 1925, an American astronomer by the name of Edwin Hubble, provided observational evidence that all galaxies are receding from one another, which implies that the universe is expanding. The expansion of the universe is now an established scientific fact. This is what the Qur'ân says regarding the nature of the universe:

We have built the Firmament with might. And We indeed have vast power. (Al-Qur'ân 51:47)

The Arabic word *Musi'ûn* is correctly translated as 'expanding it', and it refers to the creation of the expanding vastness of the universe.

Stephen Hawking, in his book, '*A Brief History of Time*', says, "The discovery that the universe is expanding was one of the great intellectual revolutions of the 20th century." The Qur'ân mentioned the expansion of the universe, before man even learnt to build a telescope!

Some may say that the presence of astronomical facts in the Qur'ân is not surprising since the Arabs were advanced in the field of astronomy. They are correct in acknowledging the advancement of the Arabs in the field of astronomy.

However they fail to realize that the Qur'ân was revealed centuries before the Arabs excelled in astronomy. Moreover, many of the scientific facts mentioned above regarding astronomy, such as the origin of the universe with a Big Bang, were not known to the Arabs even at the peak of their scientific advancement. The scientific facts mentioned in the Qur'ân are therefore not due to the Arabs' advancement in astronomy. Indeed, the reverse is true. The Arabs advanced in astronomy, because astronomy occupies a place in the Qur'ân.

The Existence of Subatomic Particles

In ancient times a well-known theory by the name of 'Theory of Atomism' was widely accepted. This theory was originally proposed by the Greeks, in particular by a man called Democritus, who lived about 23 centuries ago. Democritus and the people that came after him, assumed that the smallest unit of matter was the atom. The Arabs used to believe the same. The Arabic word *Dharrah* most commonly meant an atom.

In recent times modern science has discovered that it is possible to split even an atom. That the atom can be split further is a development of the 20th century. Fourteen centuries ago this concept would have appeared unusual even to an Arab. For him the *Dharrah* was the limit beyond which one could not go. The following Qur'ânic verse however, refuses to acknowledge this limit:

وَقَالَ ٱلَّذِينَ كَفَرُوٓاْ لَا تَأْتِينَا ٱلسَّاعَةُ قُلْ بَلَىٰ وَرَبِّي لَتَأْتِيَنَّكُمْ عَٰلِمِ ٱلْغَيْبِ لَا يَعْزُبُ عَنْهُ مِثْقَالُ ذَرَّةٍ فِي ٱلسَّمَٰوَٰتِ وَلَا فِي ٱلْأَرْضِ وَلَآ أَصْغَرُ مِن ذَٰلِكَ وَلَآ أَكْبَرُ إِلَّا فِي كِتَٰبٍ مُّبِينٍ ﴿٣﴾

The Unbelievers say, "Never to us will come the Hour": say, "Nay! But most surely, by my Lord, it will come upon you;- by Him Who knows the unseen,- from Whom is not hidden the least little atom in the Heavens or on earth: Nor is there anything less than that, or greater, but is in the record perspicuous.[1] (Al-Qur'ân 34:3)

This verse refers to the Omniscience of God, His knowledge of all things, hidden or apparent. It then goes further and says that God is aware of everything, including what is smaller or bigger than the atom. Thus the verse clearly shows that it is possible for something smaller than the atom to exist, a fact discovered only recently by modern science.

---

1. A similar message is conveyed in the Qur'ân in 10:61.

Geography

The Water Cycle

In 1580, Bernard Palissy was the first man to describe the present-day concept of 'water cycle'. He described how water evaporates from the oceans and cools to form clouds. The clouds move inland where they rise, condense and fall as rain. This water gathers as lakes and streams and flows back to the ocean in a continuous cycle. In the 7th century BC, Thales of Miletus believed that surface spray of the oceans was picked up by the wind and carried inland to fall as rain.

In earlier times people did not know the source of underground water. They thought the water of the oceans, under the effect of winds, was thrust towards the interior of the continents. They also believed that the water returned by a secret passage, or the Great Abyss. This passage is connected to the oceans and has been called the 'Tartarus', since Plato's time. Even Descartes, a great thinker of the eighteenth century, subscribed to this view. Till the nineteenth century, Aristotle's theory was prevalent. According to this theory, water was condensed in cool mountain caverns and formed underground lakes that fed springs. Today, we know that the rain water that seeps into the cracks of the ground is responsible for this.

The water cycle is described by the Qur'ân in the following verses:

$$\text{أَلَمْ تَرَ أَنَّ ٱللَّهَ أَنزَلَ مِنَ ٱلسَّمَآءِ مَآءً فَسَلَكَهُۥ يَنَٰبِيعَ فِى ٱلْأَرْضِ ثُمَّ يُخْرِجُ بِهِۦ زَرْعًا مُّخْتَلِفًا أَلْوَٰنُهُۥ}$$

Seest thou not that Allah sends down rain from the sky, and leads it through springs in the earth? Then He causes to grow, therewith, produce of various colours. (Al-Qur'ân 39:21)

وَيُنزِلُ مِنَ ٱلسَّمَآءِ مَآءً فَيُحْيِۦ بِهِ ٱلْأَرْضَ بَعْدَ مَوْتِهَآ إِنَّ فِى ذَٰلِكَ لَءَايَٰتٍ لِّقَوْمٍ يَعْقِلُونَ ۩

And He sends down rain from the sky and with it gives life to the earth after it is dead: Verily in that are signs for those who are wise. (Al-Qur'ân 30:24)

وَأَنزَلْنَا مِنَ ٱلسَّمَآءِ مَآءً بِقَدَرٍ فَأَسْكَنَّٰهُ فِى ٱلْأَرْضِ وَإِنَّا عَلَىٰ ذَهَابٍ بِهِۦ لَقَٰدِرُونَ ۩

And We send down water from the sky according to (Due) measure, and We cause it to soak in the soil; and We certainly are able to drain it off (with ease). (Al-Qur'ân 23:18)

No other text dating back 1400 years ago gives such an accurate description of the water cycle.

Winds Impregnate the Clouds

وَأَرْسَلْنَا ٱلرِّيَـٰحَ لَوَٰقِحَ فَأَنزَلْنَا مِنَ ٱلسَّمَآءِ مَآءً فَأَسْقَيْنَـٰكُمُوهُ

And We send the fecundating winds, then cause the rain to descend from the sky, therewith providing you with water (in abundance). (Al-Qur'ân 15:22)

The Arabic word used here is *Lawaqih* which is the plural of *Laqih* from *Laqaha*, which means to impregnate or fecundate. In this context, impregnate means that the wind pushes the clouds together increasing the condensation that causes lightning and thus rain. A similar description is found in the Qur'ân:

ٱللَّهُ ٱلَّذِى يُرْسِلُ ٱلرِّيَـٰحَ فَتُثِيرُ سَحَابًا فَيَبْسُطُهُ فِى ٱلسَّمَآءِ كَيْفَ يَشَآءُ وَيَجْعَلُهُ كِسَفًا فَتَرَى ٱلْوَدْقَ يَخْرُجُ مِنْ خِلَـٰلِهِۦ فَإِذَآ أَصَابَ بِهِۦ مَن يَشَآءُ مِنْ عِبَادِهِۦٓ إِذَا هُمْ يَسْتَبْشِرُونَ ﴿٤٨﴾

It is Allah Who sends the winds and they raise the clouds: then does He spread them in the sky as He wills and break them into fragments, until thou seest rain-drops issue from the midst thereof: then when He has made them reach such of His servants as He wills, behold, they do rejoice! (Al-Qur'ân 30:48)

The Qur'ânic descriptions are absolutely accurate and agree perfectly with modern data on hydrology. The water cycle is described in several verses of the Glorious Qur'ân, including 2:19, 7:57, 13:17, 25:48-49, 36:34, 50:9-11, 56:68-70, 67:30 and 86:11.

29

Geology

Mountains are like Pegs (stakes)

In geology, the phenomenon of 'folding' is a recently discovered fact. Folding is responsible for the formation of mountain ranges. The earth's crust, on which we live, is like a solid shell, while the deeper layers are hot and fluid, and thus inhospitable to any form of life. It is also known that the stability of the mountains is linked to the phenomenon of folding, for it was the folds that were to provide foundations for the reliefs that

Geologists tell us that the radius of the earth is about 3,750 miles and the crust on which we live is very thin, ranging between 1 to 30 miles. Since the crust is thin, it has a high possibility of shaking. Mountains act like stakes or tent pegs that hold the earth's crust and give it stability.

The Qur'ân contains exactly such a description in the following Verse:

$$ أَلَمْ نَجْعَلِ الْأَرْضَ مِهَادًا ۝ وَالْجِبَالَ أَوْتَادًا ۝ $$

Have We not made the earth as a wide expanse, and the mountains as pegs? (Al-Qur'ân 78:6-7)

The word *Awtâd* means stakes or pegs (like those used to anchor a tent); they are the deep foundations of geological folds.

A book named '*Earth*' is considered as a basic reference textbook on geology in many universities around the world. One of the authors of this book is Frank Press, who was the

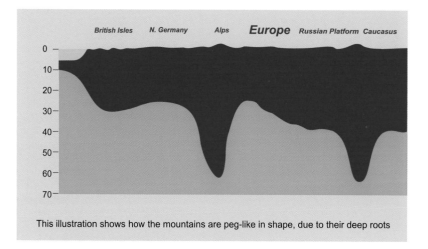

This illustration shows how the mountains are peg-like in shape, due to their deep roots

President of the Academy of Sciences in the USA for 12 years and was the Science Advisor to the former US President Jimmy Carter. In this book he illustrates the mountain in a wedge-shape and the mountain itself as a small part of the whole, whose root is deeply entrenched in the ground.[1] According to Dr. Press, the mountains play an important role in stablizing the crust of the earth.

The Qur'ân clearly mentions the function of the mountains in preventing the earth from shaking:

$$وَجَعَلْنَا فِي ٱلْأَرْضِ رَوَاسِيَ أَن تَمِيدَ بِهِمْ$$

And We have set on the earth mountains standing firm.
Al-Qur'ân 21:31)

The Qur'ânic descriptions are in perfect agreement with modern geological data.

---

1. *Earth,* Press and Siever, p. 435. Also see *Earth Science,* Tarbuck and Lutgens, p. 157.

Mountains Firmly Fixed

The surface of the earth is broken into many rigid plates that are about 100 km in thickness. These plates float on a partially molten region called asthenosphere.

Mountain formations occur at the boundary of the plates. The earth's crust is 5 km thick below oceans, about 35 km thick below flat continental surfaces and almost 80 km thick below great mountain ranges. These are the strong foundations on which mountains stand. The Qur'ân also speaks about the strong mountain foundations in the following verse:

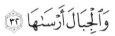

And the mountains hath He firmly fixed..[1] (Al-Qur'ân 79:32)

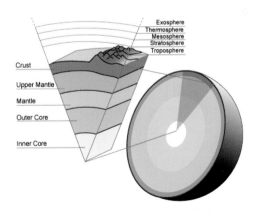

---

1. A similar message is contained in the Qur'ân in 88:19, 31:10 and 16:15.

Oceanography

Barrier between Sweet and Salt Waters

Consider the following Qur'ânic Verses:

He has let free the two seas meeting together. Between them is a barrier which they do not transgress. (Al-Qur'ân 55:19-20)

In the Arabic text the word *Barzakh* means a barrier or a partition. This barrier is not a physical partition. The Arabic word *Maraja* literally means 'they both meet and mix with each other'. Early commentators of the Qur'ân were unable to explain the two opposite meanings for the two bodies of water, i.e., they meet and mix, and at the same time, there is a barrier between them. Modern science has discovered that in the places where two different seas meet, there is a barrier between them. This barrier divides the two seas so that each sea has its own temperature, salinity and density.[1] Oceanographists are now in a better position to explain this verse. There is a slanted unseen water barrier between the two seas through which water from one sea passes to the other.

But when the water from one sea enters the other sea, it loses its distinctive characteristic and becomes homogenized with the other water. In a way this barrier serves as a transitional homogenizing area for the the two waters.

This scientific phenomenon mentioned in the Qur'ân was also confirmed by Dr. William Hay who is a well-known

---

1. *Principles of Oceanography,* Davis, pp. 92-93.

marine scientist and Professor of Geolgical Sciences at the University of Colorado, USA.

The Qur'ân mentions this phenomenon also in the following verse:

$$\text{وَجَعَلَ بَيْنَ ٱلْبَحْرَيْنِ حَاجِزًا}$$

And made a separating bar between the two seas (Can there be another). (Al-Qur'ân 27:61)

This phenomenon occurs in several places, including the divider between the Mediterranean and the Atlantic Ocean at Gibralter.

But when the Qur'ân speaks about the divider between fresh and salt water, it mentions the existence of 'a forbidding partition' with the barrier.

$$\text{وَهُوَ ٱلَّذِى مَرَجَ ٱلْبَحْرَيْنِ هَـٰذَا عَذْبٌ فُرَاتٌ وَهَـٰذَا مِلْحٌ أُجَاجٌ}$$
$$\text{وَجَعَلَ بَيْنَهُمَا بَرْزَخًا وَحِجْرًا مَّحْجُورًا ﴿٥٣﴾}$$

It is He Who has let free the two bodies of flowing water: One palatable and sweet, and the other salt and bitter; yet has He made a barrier between them, a partition that is not to be passed. (Al-Qur'ân 25:53)

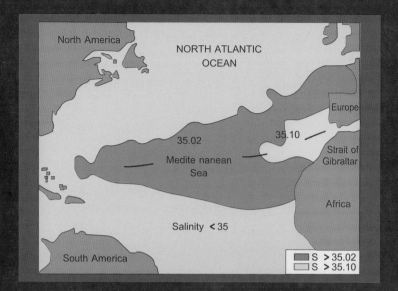

Modern science has discovered that in estuaries, where fresh (sweet) and salt water meet, the situation is somewhat different from that found in places where two seas meet. It has been discovered that what distinguishes fresh water from salt water in estuaries is a "pycnocline zone with a marked density discontinuity separating the two layers."[1] This partition (zone of separation) has a salinity different from both the fresh water and the salt water.

This phenomenon occurs in several places, including Egypt, where the river Nile flows into the Mediterranean Sea.

1. Oceanography, Gross, p. 242. Also see Introductory Oceanography, Thurman, pp. 200-201.
2. Oceanography, Gross, p.244 and introductory Oceanography, Thurman pp 200-201.

Darkness in the Depths of the Ocean

Prof. Durga Rao is an expert in the field of Marine Geology and was a professor at King Abdul Aziz University in Jeddah. He was asked to comment on the following Verse:

أَوْ كَظُلُمَتٍ فِى بَحْرٍ لُّجِّيٍّ يَغْشَىٰهُ مَوْجٌ مِّن فَوْقِهِۦ مَوْجٌ مِّن فَوْقِهِۦ سَحَابٌ ظُلُمَتٌۢ بَعْضُهَا فَوْقَ بَعْضٍ إِذَآ أَخْرَجَ يَدَهُۥ لَمْ يَكَدْ يَرَىٰهَا وَمَن لَّمْ يَجْعَلِ ٱللَّهُ لَهُۥ نُورًا فَمَا لَهُۥ مِن نُّورٍ ۝

Or (the Unbelievers' state) is like the depths of darkness in a vast deep ocean, Overwhelmed with billow topped by billow, topped by (dark) clouds: Depths of darkness, one above another: if a man stretches out his hand, he can hardly see it! For any to whom Allah giveth not light, there is no light! (Al-Qur'ân 24:40)

Prof. Rao said that scientists have only now been able to confirm, with the help of modern equipment that there is darkness in the depths of the ocean. Humans are unable to dive unaided underwater for more than 20 to 30 meters, and cannot survive in the deep oceanic regions at a depth of more than 200 meters. This verse does not refer to all seas because not every sea can be described as having accumulated darkness layered one over another. It refers especially to a deep sea or deep ocean, as the Qur'ân says, "darkness in vast deep ocean". This layered darkness in a deep ocean is the result of two causes:

1. A light ray is composed of seven colours. These seven colours are Violet, Indigo, Blue, Green, Yellow, Orange and

Red (VIBGYOR). The light ray undergoes refraction when it hits water. The upper 10 to 15 metres of water absorbs the red colour. Therefore if a diver is 25 metres under water and gets wounded, he would not be able to see the red colour of his blood, because the red colour does not reach this depth. Similarly orange rays are absorbed at 30 to 50 metres, yellow at 50 to 100 metres, green at 100 to 200 metres, and finally, blue beyond 200 metres and violet and indigo above 200 metres. Due to successive disappearance of colour, one layer after another, the ocean progressively becomes darker, i.e., darkness takes place in layers of light. Below a depth of 1000 metres there is complete darkness.

2. The sun's rays are absorbed by clouds which in turn scatter light rays thus causing a layer of darkness under the clouds. This is the first layer of darkness. When light rays reach the surface of the ocean they are reflected by the wave surface giving it a shiny appearance. Therefore it is the waves that reflect light and cause darkness. The unreflected light penetrates into the depths of the ocean. Therefore the ocean

has two parts. The surface characterized by light and warmth and the depth characterized by darkness. The surface is further separated from the deep part of the ocean by waves.

The internal waves cover the deep waters of seas and oceans because the deep waters have a higher density than the waters above them.

The darkness begins below the internal waves. Even the fish in the depths of the ocean cannot see; their only source of light is from their own bodies.

The Qur'ân rightly mentions:

"Darkness in a vast deep ocean overwhelmed with waves topped by waves".

In other words, above these waves there are more types of waves, i.e., those found on the surface of the ocean. The Qur'ânic verse continues, "topped by (dark) clouds; depths of darkness, one above another."

These clouds, as explained, are barriers one over the other that further cause darkness by absorption of colors at different levels.

Prof. Durga Rao concluded by saying, "1400 years ago a normal human being could not explain this phenomenon in so much detail. Thus the information must have come from a supernatural source".

Biology

Every Living thing is made of Water

Consider the following Qur'ânic verse:

أَوَلَمْ يَرَ ٱلَّذِينَ كَفَرُوٓاْ أَنَّ ٱلسَّمَٰوَٰتِ وَٱلْأَرْضَ كَانَتَا رَتْقًا فَفَتَقْنَٰهُمَاۖ وَجَعَلْنَا مِنَ ٱلْمَآءِ كُلَّ شَىْءٍ حَىٍّۗ أَفَلَا يُؤْمِنُونَ ٣٠

Do not the Unbelievers see that the heavens and the earth Were joined together (as one unit of Creation), before We clove them asunder? We made form water every living thing. Will they not then believe? (Al-Qur'ân 21:30)

Only after advances have been made in science, do we now know that cytoplasm, the basic substance of the cell is made up of 80% water. Modern research has also revealed that most organisms consist of 50% to 90% water and that every living entity requires water for its existence.

Was it possible 14 centuries ago for any human being to guess that every living being was made of water? Moreover would such a guess be conceivable by a human being in the deserts of Arabia where there has always been scarcity of water?

The following verse refers to the creation of animals from water:

وَٱللَّهُ خَلَقَ كُلَّ دَآبَّةٍ مِّن مَّآءٍۖ

And Allah has created every animal from water. (Al-Qur'ân 24:45)

The following verse refers to the creation of human beings from water:

وَهُوَ ٱلَّذِى خَلَقَ مِنَ ٱلْمَآءِ بَشَرًا فَجَعَلَهُ نَسَبًا وَصِهْرًا ۗ وَكَانَ رَبُّكَ قَدِيرًا ۝

It is He Who has created man from water: Then has He established relationships of lineage and marriage: for thy Lord has power (over all things). (Al-Qur'ân 25:54)

Botany

Plants created in Pairs, Male and Female

Previously humans did not know that plants too have male and female gender distinctions. Botany states that every plant has a male and female gender. Even the plants that are unisexual have distinct elements of both male and female.

وَأَنزَلَ مِنَ ٱلسَّمَآءِ مَآءً فَأَخْرَجْنَا بِهِۦ أَزْوَٰجًا مِّن نَّبَاتٍ شَتَّىٰ ﴿٥٣﴾

And has sent down water from the sky. With it We produced diverse pairs of plants each separate from the others. (Al-Qur'ân 20:53)

Fruits Created in Pairs, Male and Female

وَمِن كُلِّ ٱلثَّمَرَٰتِ جَعَلَ فِيهَا زَوْجَيْنِ ٱثْنَيْنِ

And fruit of every kind He made in pairs, two and two. (Al-Qur'ân 13:3)

Fruit is the end product of reproduction of the superior plants. The stage preceding fruit is the flower, which has male and female organs (stamens and ovules). Once pollen has been carried to the flower, they bear fruit, which in turn matures and frees its seed. All fruits therefore imply the existence of male and female organs; a fact that is mentioned in the Qur'ân.

In certain species, fruit can come from non-fertilized flowers (parenthocarpic fruit), e.g., bananas, certain types of pineapple, fig, orange, vine, etc. They also have definite sexual characteristics.

Everything made in Pairs

وَمِن كُلِّ شَيْءٍ خَلَقْنَا زَوْجَيْنِ

And of every thing We have created pairs. (Al-Qur'ân 51:49)

This refers to things other than humans, animals, plants and fruits. It may also be referring to a phenomenon like electricity in which the atoms consist of negatively- and positively-charged electrons and protons.

سُبْحَٰنَ ٱلَّذِى خَلَقَ ٱلْأَزْوَٰجَ كُلَّهَا مِمَّا تُنۢبِتُ ٱلْأَرْضُ وَمِنْ أَنفُسِهِمْ وَمِمَّا لَا يَعْلَمُونَ ﴿٣٦﴾

Glory to Allah, Who created in pairs all things that the earth produces, as well as their own (human) kind and (other) things of which they have no knowledge. (Al-Qur'ân 36:36)

The Qur'ân here says that everything is created in pairs, including things that the humans do not know at present and may discover later.

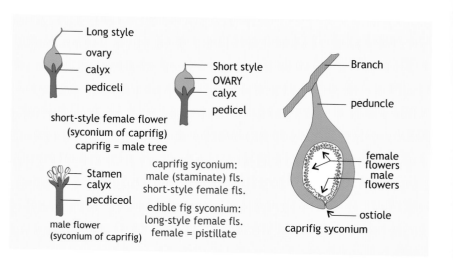

Long style
ovary
calyx
pediceli

short-style female flower
(syconium of caprifig)
caprifig = male tree

Short style
OVARY
calyx
pedicel

Branch
peduncle

female flowers
male flowers

Stamen
calyx
pecdiceol

male flower
(syconium of caprifig)

caprifig syconium:
male (staminate) fls.
short-style female fls.

edible fig syconium:
long-style female fls.
female = pistillate

ostiole
caprifig syconium

Zoology

Animals and Birds live in Communities

وَمَا مِن دَآبَّةٍ فِى ٱلْأَرْضِ وَلَا طَـٰٓئِرٍ يَطِيرُ بِجَنَاحَيْهِ إِلَّا أُمَمٌ أَمْثَالُكُم

There is not an animal (that lives) on the earth, nor a being that flies on its wings, but (forms part of) communities like you. (Al-Qur'ân 6:38)

Research has shown that animals and birds live in communities, i.e., they organize, and live and work together.

The Flight of Birds

Regarding the flight of birds, the Qur'ân says:

أَلَمْ يَرَوْاْ إِلَى ٱلطَّيْرِ مُسَخَّرَٰتٍ فِى جَوِّ ٱلسَّمَآءِ مَا يُمْسِكُهُنَّ إِلَّا ٱللَّهُ إِنَّ فِى ذَٰلِكَ لَـَٔايَـٰتٍ لِّقَوْمٍ يُؤْمِنُونَ ۝

Do they not look at the birds, held poised in the midst of (the air and) the sky? Nothing holds them up but (the power of) Allah. Verily in this are signs for those who believe. (Al-Qur'ân 16:79)

A similar message is repeated in the Qur'ân in the verse:

أَوَلَمْ يَرَوْاْ إِلَى ٱلطَّيْرِ فَوْقَهُمْ صَـٰٓفَّـٰتٍ وَيَقْبِضْنَ مَا يُمْسِكُهُنَّ إِلَّا ٱلرَّحْمَـٰنُ إِنَّهُ بِكُلِّ شَىْءٍ بَصِيرٌ ۝

Do they not observe the birds above them, spreading their wings and folding them in? None can uphold them except the Most Gracious: Truly it is He that watches over all things. (Al-Qur'ân 67:19)

The Arabic word *Amsaka* literally means, 'to put one's hand on, seize, hold, hold someone back,' which expresses the idea that Allâh holds the bird up in His power. These verses stress the extremely close dependence of the birds' behavior on Divine order. Modern scientific data has shown the degree of perfection attained by certain species of birds with regard to the programming of their movements. It is only the existence of a migratory program in the genetic code of the birds that can explain the long and complicated journey that very young birds, without any prior experience and without any guide, are able to accomplish. They are also able to return to the departure point on a definite date.

Prof. Hamburger in his book '*Power and Fragility*' gives the example of 'mutton-bird' that lives in the Pacific with its journey of over 15,000 miles in the shape of figure '8'. It makes this journey over a period of 6 months and comes back to its departure point with a maximum delay of one week. The highly complicated instructions for such a journey have to be contained in the birds' nervous cells. They are definitely programmed. Should we not reflect on the identity of this 'Programmer'?

The Bee

وَأَوْحَىٰ رَبُّكَ إِلَى ٱلنَّحْلِ أَنِ ٱتَّخِذِى مِنَ ٱلْجِبَالِ بُيُوتًا وَمِنَ ٱلشَّجَرِ
وَمِمَّا يَعْرِشُونَ ۝ ثُمَّ كُلِى مِن كُلِّ ٱلثَّمَرَٰتِ فَٱسْلُكِى سُبُلَ رَبِّكِ
ذُلُلًا

And thy Lord taught the Bee To build its cells in hills, on trees, and in (men's) habitations. Then to eat of all The produce (of the earth), and follow the ways of Thy Lord made smooth. . (Al-Qur'ân 16:68:69)

Von-Frisch received the Nobel Prize in 1973 for his research on the behaviour and communication of the bees. The bee, after discovering any new garden or flower, goes back and tells its fellow bees the exact direction and map to get there, which is known as 'bee dance'. The meanings of this insect's movements that are intended to transmit information between worker bees have been discovered scientifically using photography and other methods. The Qur'ân mentions in the above verse how the bee finds with skill the spacious paths of its Lord.

The worker bee or the soldier bee is a female bee. In *Surah An-Nahl,* chapter no. 16, Verses 68 and 69 the gender used for the bee is the female gender *(Fasluki* and *Kuli),* indicating that the bee that leaves its home for gathering food is a female bee. In other words the soldier or worker bee is a female bee.

However, in Shakespeare's play, "*Henry the Fourth*", some of the characters speak about bees and mention that the bees are soldiers and that they have a king. That is what people thought in Shakespearean times. They thought that the worker bees are male bees and they go home and are answerable to a king bee. This, however, is not true. The worker bees are females and they do not report to a king bee but to a queen bee. But it took modern investigations in the last 300 years to discover this.

Spider's Web/Home is Fragile

The Qur'ân mentions in *Surah Al-'Ankabut*,

مَثَلُ ٱلَّذِينَ ٱتَّخَذُوا۟ مِن دُونِ ٱللَّهِ أَوْلِيَآءَ كَمَثَلِ ٱلْعَنكَبُوتِ ٱتَّخَذَتْ بَيْتًا ۖ وَإِنَّ أَوْهَنَ ٱلْبُيُوتِ لَبَيْتُ ٱلْعَنكَبُوتِ ۚ لَوْ كَانُوا۟ يَعْلَمُونَ ﴿٤١﴾

The parable of those who take protectors other than Allah is that of the spider, who builds (to itself) a house; but truly the flimsiest of houses is the spider's house;- if they but knew.
(Al-Qur'ân 29:41)

Besides giving the physical description of the spider's web as being very flimsy, delicate and weak, the Qur'ân also stresses on the flimsiness of the relationship in the spider's house, where the female spider many a times kills its mate, the male spider.

Lifestyle and Communication of Ants

Consider the following Qur'ânic verse:

وَحُشِرَ لِسُلَيْمَٰنَ جُنُودُهُ مِنَ الْجِنِّ وَالْإِنسِ وَالطَّيْرِ فَهُمْ يُوزَعُونَ ۝ حَتَّىٰٓ إِذَآ أَتَوْا عَلَىٰ وَادِ النَّمْلِ قَالَتْ نَمْلَةٌ يَٰٓأَيُّهَا النَّمْلُ ادْخُلُوا مَسَٰكِنَكُمْ لَا يَحْطِمَنَّكُمْ سُلَيْمَٰنُ وَجُنُودُهُ وَهُمْ لَا يَشْعُرُونَ ۝

And before Solomon were marshalled His hosts, of Jinns and men and birds, and they were all kept in order and ranks. At length, when they came to a valley of ants, One of the ants said: "O ye ants, get into your habitations, lest Solomon and his hosts crush you (under foot) without knowing it. (Al-Qur'ân 27:17-18)

In the past, some people would have probably mocked at the Qur'ân, taking it to be a fairy tale book in which ants talk to each other and communicate sophisticated messages.

In recent times, research has shown us several facts about the lifestyle of ants, which were not known earlier to humankind. Research has shown that the animals or insects whose lifestyle is closest in resemblance to the lifestyle of human beings are the ants. This can be seen from the following findings regarding ants:

(a) The ants bury their dead in a manner similar to the humans.

(b) They have a sophisticated system of division of labour, whereby they have managers, supervisors, foremen, workers, etc.

(c) Once in a while they meet among themselves to have a 'chat'.

(d) They have an advanced method of communication among themselves.

(e) They hold regular markets wherein they exchange goods.

(f) They store grains for long periods in winter and if the grain begins to bud, they cut the roots, as if they understand that if they leave it to grow, it will rot. If the grains stored by them get wet due to rains, they take these grains out into the sunlight to dry, and once these are dry, they take them back inside as though they know that humidity will cause development of root systems and thereafter rotting of the grain.

Honey has Healing Properties

The bee assimilates juices of various kinds of flowers and fruit and forms within its body the honey, which it stores in its cells of wax. Only a couple of centuries ago, man came to know that honey comes from the belly of the bee. This fact was mentioned in the Qur'ân 1400 years ago in the following Verse:

يَخْرُجُ مِنْ بُطُونِهَا شَرَابٌ مُّخْتَلِفٌ أَلْوَنُهُ فِيهِ شِفَآءٌ لِّلنَّاسِ

There issues from within their bodies a drink of varying colours, wherein is healing for men. (Al-Qur'ân 16:69)

We are now aware that honey has a healing property and also a mild antiseptic property. The Russians used honey to cover their wounds in World War II. The wound would retain moisture and would leave very little scar tissue. Due to the density of honey, no fungus or bacteria would grow in the wound.

A person suffering from an allergy of a particular plant may be given honey from that plant so that the person develops resistance to that allergy. Honey is rich in fructose and vitamin K.

Thus the knowledge contained in the Qur'ân regarding honey, its origin and properties, was far ahead of the time it was revealed.

Physiology

Blood Circulation and the Production of Milk

The Qur'ân was revealed 600 years before the Muslim scientist Ibn Nafees described the circulation of the blood and 1000 years before William Harwey brought this understanding to the Western world. Roughly thirteen centuries before it was known what happens in the intestines to ensure that organs are nourished by the process of digestive absorption, a verse in the Qur'ân described the source of the constituents of milk, in conformity with these notions.

To understand the Qur'ânic verse concerning the above concepts, it is important to know that chemical reactions occur in the intestines and that, from there, substances extracted from food pass into the blood stream via a complex system; sometimes by way of the liver, depending on their chemical nature. The blood transports them to all the organs of the body, among which are the milk-producing mammary glands.

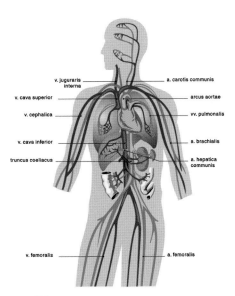

In simple terms, certain substances from the

contents of the intestines enter into the vessels of the intestinal wall itself, and these substances are transported by the blood stream to the various organs.

This concept must be fully appreciated if we wish to understand the following verses in the Qur'ân:

وَإِنَّ لَكُمْ فِي ٱلْأَنْعَٰمِ لَعِبْرَةً نُّسْقِيكُم مِّمَّا فِي بُطُونِهِۦ مِنۢ بَيْنِ فَرْثٍ وَدَمٍ لَّبَنًا خَالِصًا سَآئِغًا لِّلشَّٰرِبِينَ ﴿٦٦﴾

And verily in cattle (too) will ye find an instructive Sign. From what is within their bodies, between excretions and blood, We produce, for your drink, milk, pure and agreeable to those who drink it. (Al-Qur'ân 16:66) [1]

وَإِنَّ لَكُمْ فِي ٱلْأَنْعَٰمِ لَعِبْرَةً نُّسْقِيكُم مِّمَّا فِي بُطُونِهَا وَلَكُمْ فِيهَا مَنَٰفِعُ كَثِيرَةٌ وَمِنْهَا تَأْكُلُونَ ﴿٢١﴾

And in cattle (too) ye have an instructive example: From within their bodies We produce (milk) for you to drink; there are, in them, (Besides), numerous (other) benefits for you; and of their (meat) ye eat. (Al-Qur'ân 23:21)

The Qur'ânic description of the production of milk in cattle is strikingly similar to what modern physiology has discovered.

---

1. Translation of this Qur'ânic Verse is from the book "*The Bible, the Qur'ân and Science*" by Dr. Maurice Bucaille.

Embryology

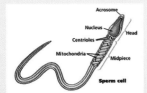

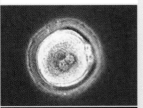

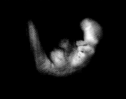

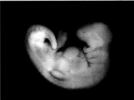

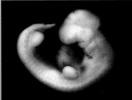

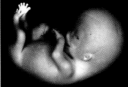

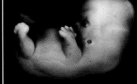

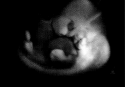

Man is created from 'Alaq
—a Leech-like Substance

A few years ago a group of Arabs collected all information concerning embryology from the Qur'ân and followed the instruction of the Qur'ân:

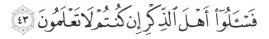

If ye realise this not, ask of those who possess the Message.
(Al-Qur'ân 16:43 & 21:7)

All the information from the Qur'ân so gathered, was translated into English and presented to Prof. (Dr.) Keith Moore, who was the Professor of Embryology and Chairman of the Department of Anatomy at the University of Toronto, in Canada. At present he is one of the highest authorities in the field of embryology.

He was asked to give his opinion regarding the information present in the Qur'ân concerning the field of embryology. After carefully examining the translation of the Qur'ânic verses presented to him, Dr. Moore said that most of the information concerning embryology mentioned in the Qur'ân is in perfect conformity with modern discoveries in the field of embryology and does not conflict with them in any way. He added that there were however a few verses, on whose scientific accuracy he could not comment. He could not say whether the statements were true or false, since he himself was not aware of the information contained therein. There was also no mention of this information in modern writings and studies on embryology. One such verse is:

اقْرَأْ بِٱسْمِ رَبِّكَ ٱلَّذِى خَلَقَ ١ خَلَقَ ٱلْإِنسَٰنَ مِنْ عَلَقٍ ٢

Proclaim! (Or Read!) In the name of thy Lord and Cherisher, Who created. Created man, out of a leech-like clot. (Al-Qur'ân 96:1-2)

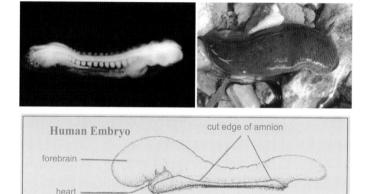

The word 'Alaq besides meaning a congealed clot of blood also means something that clings, a leech-like substance.

Dr. Keith Moore had no knowledge whether an embryo in the initial stages appears like a leech. To check this out he studied the initial stage of the embryo under a very powerful microscope in his laboratory and compared what he observed with a diagram of a leech and he was astonished at the striking resemblance between the two!

In the same manner, he acquired more information on embryology, that was hitherto not known to him, from the Qur'ân.

Dr. Keith Moore answered about eighty questions dealing with embryological data mentioned in the Qur'ân and Hadith. Noting that the information contained in the Qur'ân and Hadith was in full agreement with the latest discoveries in the field of embryology, Prof. Moore said, "If I was asked these questions thirty years ago, I would not have been able to answer half of them for lack of scientific information."

Dr. Keith Moore had earlier authored the book, 'The Developing Human'. After acquiring new knowledge from the Qur'ân, he wrote, in 1982, the 3rd edition of the same book, 'The Developing Human'. The book was the recipient of an award for the best medical book written by a single author. This book has been translated into several major languages of the world and is used as a textbook of embryology in the first year of medical studies.

In 1981, during the Seventh Medical Conference in Dammam, Saudi Arabia, Dr. Moore said, "It has been a great pleasure for me to help clarify statements in the Qur'ân about human development. It is clear to me that these statements must have come to Muhammad from God or Allâh, because almost all of this knowledge was not discovered until many centuries later. This proves to me that Muhammad must have been a Messenger of God or Allâh."[1]

Dr. Joe Leigh Simpson, Chairman of the Department of Obstetrics and Gynecology, at the Baylor College of Medicine, Houston, USA, proclaims "these *Ahadith*, sayings of Muhammad (ﷺ) could not have been obtained on the basis of the scientific knowledge that was available at the time of the writer (7th century). It follows that not only is there no conflict between genetics and religion (Islam) but in

1. The reference for this statement is the video tape titled *"This is the Truth"*. For a copy of this video tape contact the Islamic Research Foundation.

fact religion (Islam) may guide science by adding revelation to some of the traditional scientific approaches... there exist statements in the Qur'ân shown centuries later to be valid which support knowledge in the Qur'ân having been derived from God."

Man Created from a drop emitted from between the Backbone and the Ribs

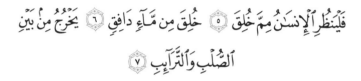

Now let man but think from what he is created! He is created from a drop emitted. Proceeding from between the backbone and the ribs.. (Al-Qur'ân 86:5-7)

In embryonic stages, the reproductive organs of the male and female, i.e., the testicles and the ovaries, begin their development near the kidney between the spinal column and the eleventh and twelfth ribs. Later they descend; the female gonads (ovaries) stop in the pelvis while the male gonads (testicles) continue their descent before birth to reach the scrotum through the inguinal canal. Even in the adult after the descent of the reproductive organ, these organs receive their nerve supply and blood supply from the abdominal aorta, which is in the area between the backbone (spinal column) and the ribs. Even the lymphatic drainage and the venous return go to the same area.

Human Beings created from *Nutfah* (Minute Quantity of Liquid)

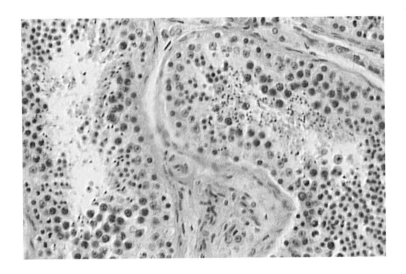

The Glorious Qur'ân mentions no less than eleven times that the human being is created from *Nutfah*, which means a minute quantity of liquid or a trickle of liquid which remains after emptying a cup. This is mentioned in several verses of the Qur'ân including 22:5 and 23:13.[1]

Science has confirmed in recent times that only one out of an average of three million ejaculated sperms is required for fertilizing the ovum. This means that only a 1/three millionth part or 0.00003% of the quantity of ejaculated sperms that are emitted is required for fertilization.

---

1. The same is also mentioned in the Qur'an in 16:4, 18:37, 35:11, 36:77, 40:67, 53:46, 75:37, 76:2 and 80:19.

Human Beings created from *Sulâlah* (Quintessence of Liquid)

And made his progeny from a quintessence of despised fluid. (Al-Qur'ân 32:8)

The Arabic word *Sulâlah* means quintessence or the best part of a whole. We have come to know now that only one single spermatozoon that penetrates the ovum is required for fertilization, out of the several millions produced by man. That one spermatozoon out of several millions, is referred to in the Qur'ân as *Sulâlah*. *Sulâlah* also means gentle extraction from a fluid. The fluid refers to both male and female germinal fluids containing gametes. Both ovum and sperm are gently extracted from their environments in the process of fertilization.

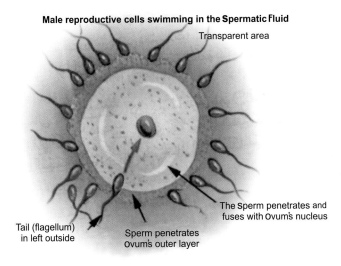

Male reproductive cells swimming in the Spermatic Fluid

Transparent area

Tail (flagellum) in left outside

Sperm penetrates Ovum's outer layer

The Sperm penetrates and fuses with Ovum's nucleus

Man created from *Nutfatun Amshâj* (Mingled Liquids)

Consider the following Qur'ânic Verse:

إِنَّا خَلَقْنَا ٱلْإِنسَٰنَ مِن نُّطْفَةٍ أَمْشَاجٍ

Verily We created Man from a drop of mingled sperm. (Al-Qur'ân 76:2)

The Arabic word *Nutfatin Amshâjin* means mingled liquids. According to some commentators of the Qur'ân, mingled liquids refer to the male or female agents or liquids. After mixture of male and female gamete, the zygote still remains *Nutfah*. Mingled liquids can also refer to spermatic fluid that is formed of various secretions that come from various glands.

Therefore *Nutfatin Amshâj*, i.e., a minute quantity of mingled fluids refers to the male and female gametes (germinal fluids or cells) and part of the surrounding fluids.

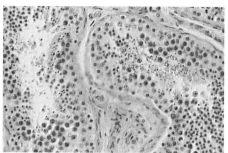
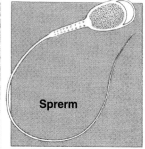

Sprerm

Sex Determination

The sex of a foetus is determined by the nature of the sperm and not the ovum. The sex of the child, whether female or male, depends on whether the 23rd pair of chromosomes is XX or XY respectively.

Primarily sex determination occurs at fertilization and depends upon the type of sex chromosome in the sperm that fertilizes an ovum. If it is an 'X' bearing sperm that fertilizes the ovum, the foetus is a female and if it is a 'Y' bearing sperm then the foetus is a male.

وَأَنَّهُۥ خَلَقَ ٱلزَّوْجَيْنِ ٱلذَّكَرَ وَٱلْأُنثَىٰ ﴿٤٥﴾ مِن نُّطْفَةٍ إِذَا تُمْنَىٰ ﴿٤٦﴾

That He did create the pairs, - male and female, from a sperm-drop when lodged (in its place). (Al-Qur'ân 53:45-46)

The Arabic word *Nutfah* means a minute quantity of liquid and *Tumna* means ejaculated or planted. Therefore *Nutfah* specifically refers to sperm because it is ejaculated.

The Qur'ân says:

أَلَمْ يَكُ نُطْفَةً مِّن مَّنِيٍّ يُمْنَىٰ ﴿٣٧﴾ ثُمَّ كَانَ عَلَقَةً فَخَلَقَ فَسَوَّىٰ ﴿٣٨﴾ فَجَعَلَ مِنْهُ ٱلزَّوْجَيْنِ ٱلذَّكَرَ وَٱلْأُنثَىٰ ﴿٣٩﴾

Was he not a drop of sperm emitted (in lowly form)? Then did (Allah) make and fashion (him) in due proportion. And of him He made two sexes, male and female. (Al-Qur'ân 75:37-39)

Here again it is mentioned that a small quantity (drop) of sperm (indicated by the word *Nutfatan min Maniyyin*) which comes from the man is responsible for the sex of the foetus.

Mothers-in-law in the Indian subcontinent, by and large prefer having male grandchildren and often blame their daughters-in-law if the child is not of the desired sex. If only they knew that the determining factor is the nature of the male sperm and not the female ovum! If they were to blame anybody, they should blame their sons and not their daughters-in-law since both the Qur'ân and science hold that it is the male fluid that is responsible for the sex of the child!

Foetus protected by three Veils of Darkness

$$\text{يَخْلُقُكُمْ فِي بُطُونِ أُمَّهَٰتِكُم خَلْقًا مِّنۢ بَعْدِ خَلْقٍ فِي ظُلُمَٰتٍ ثَلَٰثٍ}$$

He creates you, in the wombs of your mothers, in stages, one after another, In three veils of darkness. (Al-Qur'ân 39:6)

According to Prof. Keith Moore these three veils of darkness in the Qur'ân refer to:

(i) anterior abdominal wall of the mother

(ii) the uterine wall

(iii) the amnio-chorionic membrane.

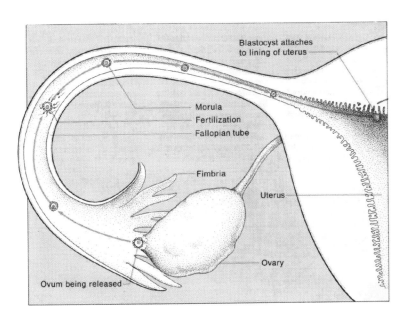

Blastocyst attaches to lining of uterus

Morula

Fertilization

Fallopian tube

Fimbria

Uterus

Ovary

Ovum being released

Embryonic Stages

وَلَقَدْ خَلَقْنَا ٱلْإِنسَـٰنَ مِن سُلَـٰلَةٍ مِّن طِينٍ ۝ ثُمَّ جَعَلْنَـٰهُ
نُطْفَةً فِي قَرَارٍ مَّكِينٍ ۝ ثُمَّ خَلَقْنَا ٱلنُّطْفَةَ عَلَقَةً فَخَلَقْنَا
ٱلْعَلَقَةَ مُضْغَةً فَخَلَقْنَا ٱلْمُضْغَةَ عِظَـٰمًا فَكَسَوْنَا
ٱلْعِظَـٰمَ لَحْمًا ثُمَّ أَنشَأْنَـٰهُ خَلْقًا ءَاخَرَ فَتَبَارَكَ ٱللَّهُ أَحْسَنُ
ٱلْخَـٰلِقِينَ ۝

Man We did create from a quintessence (of clay), then We placed him as (a drop of) sperm in a place of rest, firmly fixed; Then We made the sperm into a clot of congealed blood, then of that clot We made a (foetus) lump; then We made out of that lump bones and clothed the bones with flesh; then We developed out of it another creature. So blessed be Allah, the Best of create! (Al-Qur'ân 23:12-14)

In this verse Allâh states that man is created from a small quantity of liquid which is placed in a place of rest, firmly fixed (well established or lodged) for which the Arabic word *Qarârin Makin* is used. The uterus is well protected from the posterior by the spinal column supported firmly by the back muscles. The embryo is further protected by the amniotic sac containing the amniotic fluid. Thus the foetus has a well-protected dwelling place.

This small quantity of fluid is made into *'Alaqah*, meaning something that clings. It also means a leech-like substance. Both descriptions are scientifically acceptable as in the very early stages the foetus clings to the wall and also appears to resemble the leech in shape. It also behaves like a leech (blood sucker) and acquires its blood supply from the mother through the placenta.

The third meaning of the word *'Alaqah* is a blood clot. During this *'Alaqah* stage, which spans the third and fourth week of pregnancy, the blood clots within closed vessels. Hence the embryo acquires the appearance of a blood clot in addition to acquiring the appearance of a leech.

In 1677, Hamm and Leeuwenhoek were the first scientists to observe human sperm cells (spermatozoa) using a microscope. They thought that a sperm cell contained a miniature human being that grew in the uterus to form a newborn. This was known as the perforation theory. When scientists discovered that the ovum was bigger than the sperm, it was thought by De Graf and others that the foetus existed in a miniature form in the ovum. Later, in the 18th century Maupertuis propagated the theory of biparental inheritance.

The 'Alaqah is transformed into Mudghah which means 'something that is chewed (having teeth marks)' and also something that is tacky and small, which can be put in the mouth like gum. Both these explanations are scientifically correct. Prof. Keith Moore took a piece of plaster seal and made it into the size and shape of the early stage of foetus and chewed it between the teeth to make it into a 'Mudghah'. He compared this with the photographs of the early stage of foetus. The teeth marks resembled the 'somites' which is the early formation of the spinal column.

This Mudghah is transformed into bones (Izâm). The bones

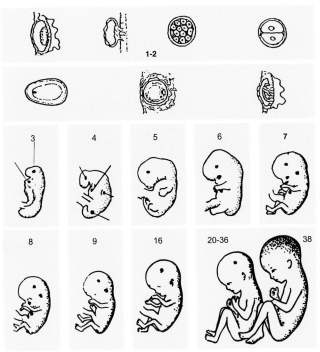

are clothed with intact flesh or muscles *(Lahm)*. Then Allâh makes it into another creature.

Prof. Marshall Johnson is one of the leading scientists in US, and is the head of the Department of Anatomy and Director of the Daniel Institute at the Thomas Jefferson University in Philadelphia in the US. He was asked to comment on the verses of the Qur'ân dealing with embryology. He said that the verses of the Qur'ân describing the embryological stages cannot be a coincidence. He said it was probable that Muhammad (ﷺ) had a powerful microscope. On being reminded that the Qur'ân was revealed 1400 years ago, and microscopes were invented centuries after the time of Prophet Muhammad (pbuh), Prof. Johnson laughed and admitted that the first microscope invented could not magnify more than 10 times and could not show a clear picture.

Later he said: "I see nothing here in conflict with the concept that Divine intervention was involved when Muhammad (ﷺ) recited the Qur'ân."

According to Dr. Keith Moore, the modern classification of embryonic development stages that is adopted throughout the world, is not easily comprehensible, since it identifies stages on a numerical basis, i.e., stage I, stage II, etc. The divisions revealed in the Qur'ân are based on distinct and easily identifiable forms or shapes, which the embryo passes through. These are based on different phases of prenatal development and provide elegant scientific descriptions that are comprehensible and practical.

Similar embryological stages of human development have been described in the following verses:

أَلَمْ يَكُ نُطْفَةً مِّن مَّنِيٍّ يُمْنَىٰ ۝ ثُمَّ كَانَ عَلَقَةً فَخَلَقَ فَسَوَّىٰ ۝ فَجَعَلَ مِنْهُ الزَّوْجَيْنِ الذَّكَرَ وَالْأُنثَىٰ ۝

Was he not a drop of sperm emitted (In lowly form)? Then did he become a leach-like clot; then did (Allah) make and fashion (him) in due proportion. And of him He made two sexes, male and female. (Al-Qur'ân 75:37-39)

الَّذِى خَلَقَكَ فَسَوَّىٰكَ فَعَدَلَكَ ۝ فِى أَىِّ صُورَةٍ مَّا شَاءَ رَكَّبَكَ ۝

Him Who created thee, fashioned thee in due proportion, and gave thee a just bias; in whatever form He wills, does He put thee together. (Al-Qur'ân 82:7-8)

Embryo Partly Formed and Partly Unformed

At the *Mugdhah* stage, if an incision is made in the embryo and the internal organ is dissected, it will be seen that most of them are formed while the others are not yet completely formed.

According to Prof. Johnson, if we describe the embryo as a complete creation, then we are only describing that part which is already created. If we describe it as an incomplete creation, then we are only describing that part which is not yet created. So, is it a complete creation or an incomplete creation? There is no better description of this stage of embryogenesis than the Qur'ânic description, "partly formed and partly unformed", as in the following verse:

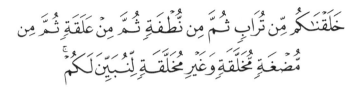

We created you out of dust, then out of sperm, then out of a leech-like clot, then out of a morsel of flesh, partly formed and partly unformed. (Al-Qur'ân 22:5)

Scientifically we know that at this early stage of development there are some cells that are differentiated and there are some cells that are undifferentiated – some organs are formed and yet others unformed.

Sense of Hearing and Sight

The first sense to develop in a developing human embryo is hearing. The foetus can hear sounds after the 24th week. Subsequently, the sense of sight is developed and by the 28th week, the retina becomes sensitive to light.

Consider the following Qur'ânic verses related to the development of the senses in the embryo:

And He gave you (the faculties of) hearing and sight and understanding. (Al-Qur'ân 32:9)

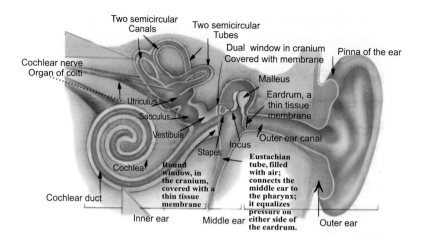

Two semicircular Canals
Two semicircular Tubes
Dual window in cranium Covered with membrane
Pinna of the ear
Cochlear nerve
Organ of coiti
Malleus
Eardrum, a thin tissue membrane
Utriculus
Sacculus
Vestibule
Outer ear canal
Incus
Stapes
Cochlea
Round window, in the cranium, covered with a thin tissue membrane
Eustachian tube, filled with air; connects the middle ear to the pharynx; it equalizes pressure on either side of the eardrum.
Cochlear duct
Inner ear
Middle ear
Outer ear

إِنَّا خَلَقْنَا ٱلْإِنسَـٰنَ مِن نُّطْفَةٍ أَمْشَاجٍ نَّبْتَلِيهِ فَجَعَلْنَـٰهُ سَمِيعًۢا بَصِيرًا ﴿٢﴾

Verily We created Man from a drop of mingled sperm, in order to try him: So We gave him (the gifts), of hearing and sight. (Al-Qur'ân 76:2)

وَهُوَ ٱلَّذِىٓ أَنشَأَ لَكُمُ ٱلسَّمْعَ وَٱلْأَبْصَـٰرَ وَٱلْأَفْـِٔدَةَ قَلِيلًا مَّا تَشْكُرُونَ ﴿٧٨﴾

It is He Who has created for you (the faculties of) hearing, sight, feeling and understanding: little thanks it is ye give! (Al-Qur'ân 23:78)

In all these verses the sense of hearing is mentioned before that of sight. Thus the Qur'ânic description matches with the discoveries in modern embryology.

General Science

Fingerprints

$$\text{أَيَحْسَبُ ٱلْإِنسَـٰنُ أَلَّن نَّجْمَعَ عِظَامَهُ ۝ بَلَىٰ قَـٰدِرِينَ عَلَىٰٓ أَن نُّسَوِّىَ بَنَانَهُ ۝}$$

Does man think that We cannot assemble his bones? Nay, We are able to put together in perfect order the very tips of his fingers. (Al-Qur'ân 75:3-4)

Unbelievers argue regarding resurrection taking place after bones of dead people have disintegrated in the earth and how each individual would be identified on the Day of Judgment. Almighty Allâh answers that He can not only assemble our bones but can also reconstruct perfectly our very fingertips.

Why does the Qur'ân, while speaking about determination of the identity of the individual, speak specifically about fingertips? In 1880, fingerprinting became the scientific method of identification, after research done by Sir Francis Golt. No two persons in the world can ever have exactly the same fingerprint pattern. That is the reason why police forces worldwide use fingerprints to identify the criminal.

1400 years ago, who could have known the uniqueness of each human's fingerprint? Surely it could have been none other than the Creator Himself!

Pain Receptors present in the Skin

It was thought that the sense of feeling and pain was only dependent on the brain. Recent discoveries prove that there are pain receptors present in the skin without which a person would not be able to feel pain.

When a doctor examines a patient suffering from burn injuries, he verifies the degree of burns by a pinprick. If the patient feels pain, the doctor is happy, because it indicates that the burns are superficial and the pain receptors are intact. On the other hand if the patient does not feel any pain, it indicates that it is a deep burn and the pain receptors have been destroyed.

The Qur'ân gives an indication of the existence of pain receptors in the following verse:

إِنَّ ٱلَّذِينَ كَفَرُواْ بِـَٔايَـٰتِنَا سَوْفَ نُصْلِيهِمْ نَارًا كُلَّمَا نَضِجَتْ جُلُودُهُم بَدَّلْنَـٰهُمْ جُلُودًا غَيْرَهَا لِيَذُوقُواْ ٱلْعَذَابَ إِنَّ ٱللَّهَ كَانَ عَزِيزًا حَكِيمًا ٥٦

Those who reject Our Signs. We shall soon cast into the Fire: As often as their skins are roasted through. We shall change them for fresh skins, that they may taste the chastisement: for Allah is Exalted in Power, Wise. (Al-Qur'ân 4:56)

Prof. Tagatat Tejasen, Chairman of the Department of Anatomy at Chiang Mai University in Thailand, has spent a great amount of time on research of pain receptors. Initially he could not believe that the Qur'ân mentioned this scientific fact 1400 years ago. He later verified the translation of this particular Qur'ânic verse. Prof. Tejasen was so impressed by the scientific accuracy of the Qur'ânic verse, that at the 8th Saudi Medical Conference held in Riyadh on the Scientific Signs of Qur'ân and *Sunnah* he proclaimed in public:

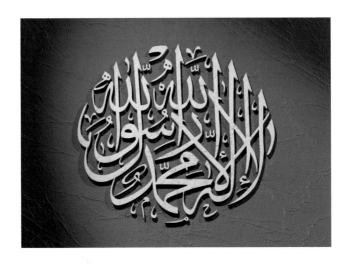

لاَ إِلَهَ إِلاَّ اللهُ مُحَمَّدٌ رَّسُوْلُ اللهِ

"There is no god but Allâh and Muhammad (ﷺ) is His Messenger."

Conclusion

To attribute the presence of scientific facts in the Qur'ân to coincidence, would be against common sense and a true scientific approach. The Qur'ân invites all humans to reflect on the Creation of this universe in the Verse:

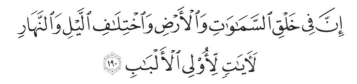

Behold! In the creation of the heavens and the earth, and the alternation of Night and Day, there are indeed Signs for men of understanding. (Al-Qur'ân 3:190)

The scientific evidences of the Qur'ân clearly prove its Divine origin. No human could have produced a book, fourteen hundred years ago, that would contain profound scientific facts, to be discovered by humankind centuries later.

The Qur'ân however, is not a book of Science but a book of 'Signs'. These signs invite Man to realize the purpose of his existence on earth, and to live in harmony with Nature. The Qur'ân is truly a message from Allâh, the Creator and Sustainer of the universe. It contains the same message of the Oneness of God, that was preached by all Prophets, right from Adam, Moses, Jesus to Muhammad (peace be upon them).

Several detailed tomes have been written on the subject of Qur'ân and modern science and further research in this field is on. *In sha' Allâh* (if Allâh wills), this research will help mankind to come close to the Word of the Almighty. This booklet contains only a few of the scientific facts present in the Qur'ân. I cannot claim to have done full justice to the subject.

Prof. Tejasen accepted Islam on the strength of just one scientific 'sign' mentioned in the Qur'ân. Some people may require ten signs while some may require hundred signs to be convinced about the Divine origin of the Qur'ân. Some would be unwilling to accept the Truth even after being shown a thousand signs. The Qur'ân condemns such a closed mentality in the verse:

صُمٌّ بُكۡمٌ عُمۡىٌ فَهُمۡ لَا يَرۡجِعُونَ ۝

Deaf, dumb, and blind, they will not return (to the path). (Al-Qur'ân 2:18)

The Qur'ân contains a complete code of life for the individual and society. *Alhamdulillâh* (praise is to Allâh), the Qur'ânic way of life is far superior to the 'isms' that modern man has invented out of sheer ignorance. Who can give better guidance than the Creator Himself?

I pray that this humble effort is accepted by Allâh, to Whom I pray for mercy and guidance (*Âmin*).